Flame in a Stable

ARROWSMITH
PRESS

Flame in a Stable
Martin Edmunds

© 2021 Martin Edmunds
All Rights Reserved

ISBN: 978-1-7376156-2-0

Boston — New York — San Francisco — Baghdad
San Juan — Kyiv — Istanbul — Santiago, Chile
Beijing — Paris — London — Cairo — Madrid
Milan — Melbourne — Jerusalem — Darfur

11 Chestnut St.
Medford, MA 02155

arrowsmithpress@gmail.com
www.arrowsmithpress.com

The thirty-eighth Arrowsmith book
was typeset & designed by Ezra Fox
for Askold Melnyczuk & Alex Johnson
in PT Serif typeface

Flame in a Stable

MARTIN EDMUNDS

Contents

I
Blocked   3

Personal Mythology   6

The Twenty-Twentieth Year of Our Lord   8

Red-Winged Blackbird Count   11

Dawn   12

Perfect Match   13

II
Boca Negra   17

The Backlook   22

Anno Domini 1999   24

Inheritance   31

The Climb   33

The D.T.'s   36

III
Petra   41

Aubade   42

Vespers   44

Can't Anyone Untie Us?   46

Ice   47

Truro/Angers, Anjou   48

Morpho   49

Chez Nous   52

Crowes Pasture   54

IV
Winterreise   59

Ocean   60

African Funeral, Anjou   62

Tetragrammaton   63

How Quietly, How Quickly   64

Metamorphosis   69

Waking   73

V
For Johnny   77

I

Blocked

Tight as a bolt
in a priest hole

hammered sidewise in—
no room

for the rumored soul,
stitched into the prison of your skin.

Whose moon face bobs wobbling up
rising through silvery fathoms

till plump lips bump the glassy
skin of the meniscus,

mouthing your name while you
freeze on the brink in a lather?

No one could be further
from the truth of you.

Is it him?
Who hit the mute

on your remote?
Who thumbs the fader

till your screen goes dim?
Is he your future

haint? You're his
parasitic twin? Unkindest

cut—that wit's
corrosive sublimate

rubbed rawly in:
Nothing new for twenty

centuries! Last year's palm is still
this year's ash.

Deus lo volt!

Fog gropes onshore like clockwork, swaddles
St. Aidan's bells in fleece

by 3 pm.
Now comes the blind shearer

through the mirror.
What has he done with your razor?

You're the reek
of spraints

in the holt,
he's fernflesh hiding

in a lightning bolt.

*

A pen would be heaven.

No pencil stub, no chalk, no
knuckle of peeled keel,

no scrap, no scratch,
no parchment paper left after

buttering their slits and tucking the gutted
trout in the oven.

How to get word out
past that armed guard

who kneels to thrawn
insomniac gods

and is wearing a mask of your face
into his flesh?

Twenty centuries in,
blood chooses thorns

to scribble its petitions on the skin.

Personal Mythology

You're Adam. She's Eve.
You fuck up: cannot conceive

Yahweh's anger. Cast east,
weep, nightly thieve then grieve

the apple back upon the bough
law proffers but does not allow.

Stand. Raise your eyes and taste
forbidden fruit, the crimson-streaked

flesh, blood, Christ-laced
salvation swallowed with the bait,

Lucifer's candescent hate.
The dove, the dove is razor-beaked.

The rosy dawn descends from her.
You're the whited sepulchre.

A waxworks sweetness rots the hives.
Hang for a sheep, hang for a goat—

How many bellies? Two newborns.
Love irrupts into your lives

—How many *bellies*? Thistles and thorns.
Tiller, shepherd, two sons set

the darkness thrumming. Whetstones, knives.
Gardener, gardener, learn your craft:

rootstock, scion, scalpel, graft
the redbud on the Jesse tree,

a Galilean ministry.
No force of nature now can stanch

the petals streaming from the branch.

The Twenty-Twentieth Year of Our Lord

Your shepherd counts our heads and hooks his flock
Indian file through the lych gate.
Reapers harvest shards of flint and slate.
No time to catch our breath or punch the clock.
Goodbye, green side of the earth!
Goodnight, daylight.
A flick of the aspergillum and it's done:
the cup of nuclear winter for one,
followed by a main of perpetual night.
But who can tell us if Catullus was right?
Does our sullen sun
set once, forever?
Or do our spirits live, streaming Godward,
mustard seeds that pass St. Peter's sieve?
But fail his riddle, and soul's fate's to be
hopped in the bonfire for eternity?

*

Your death's spreading shock waves buffet the sun,
cousin, as your final knell is rung,
colliding with the sirens in my head.
They strike against my temples, tilt
St. John's steeple level with the roof.
The swinging bellmouth lifts
the sea's rim with it—
from Throggs Neck past Belle Terre to Poquatuck
it tips the salt waves from Long Island Sound,
scrapes a basin for these tears I'm weeping now.

Would the dark god
loosen your tongue, cousin, could I pour
libations on your common grave
excavated by a Cat D4?
Are his arms gentler
than that rough god's, who bore
your wife from you when
they rolled your stretcher through the bedroom door?
Forgive us, cousin.
Rain ticks a real-time
readout of the seconds
you have left
behind, stranded
in the hallway
by the window looking on
the middle of Hell's Kitchen, yet
a stone's throw from Hart Island's rocky shore.

*

    Many who love you
    are gathered in one room,
    courtesy of Zoom.

    Lit wicks
    of lilies flicker, vigil
    candles mantle

    white wings
    against the backward
    smudge of gloom.

    A gust of light.
    Rosa holds
    a wedding photo—

you—my God, Tony! golden,
what were we,
twenty-four?

Your face flares
and dims and lives
on air.

Fuck tears. Toss salt,
I'll meet you there.

Red-Winged Blackbird Count
Herring Estuary, 2020

Twin fledglings
and no wife:
my life is looseleaf
and purple strife.

I'm that male in a mist net trilling
to the wind on the river, the light in the sky.
Males and females around me calling
Check! Check! Check! Check! Check!
Talk about boring! I don't want to die.

Dawn

No matter where I look,
your feet have preceded me.

Bells toll
the null hours.

Light enough now to see
your absence,
its enormity.

Hawk floats
out of the sun.

Flitting siskins
sketch and erase
a draft of flight under the pines.

You are everywhere.
You are everywhere.

It's going to go on like this.

Perfect Match

for Red

Me: drypoint lover.
Your brush? Loaded with color.

Me: rustic, trudging
through mud from cattail to cane-
brake, hayfoot, strawfoot, hayfoot, straw,
willing and able.

And you, my vixen?
You pour through grassland like
whiskey over ice.
Cool but kind. Kind but not nice.

A real dame
raised you to be neither
grateful nor un-
grateful. Giddy.

Brilliant. Safe
as a flame in a stable—

II

Boca Negra

Little lizard, little lizard
with your eyes sewn open
and your lips stitched tight,
was it the sun you struck
with your tongue and swallowed
or was it the night?

Your puttysack gut slung
down like a truncheon,
a blackjack, a sock
weighted with pesos
to whack the heads off jimson
or bribe the border guard.

The ignition
coil of your tail
twitched, and you moved
like a lit fuse through
these hills the slow
explosions ripped apart.

Sun-arrow,
earth-dart,
your work was murder,
enforcing
a no-fly zone.
Deep cover
Black Ops
master sergeant,
unseen, all-seeing
from your stakeout
in the schist,

under the chips
of obsidian, above
the pumice, your eye
petrified, a drop
of fossil water
from the Pleistocene.
Dead, you commune with these
mortal enemies:
it is the flies
who tithe
your measly feast.
O Boca Negra,
O my black-tongued bell
mouth soldered shut,
once, your wedge-head cut
a neat cuneiform
you had to erase with your tail:
livewire, whipstock-swipple,
lash of the sandstorm.

Quicksilver digit,
O my morning star,
your little, mimic
hands have traveled far
to end up where
the hours are sanded down,
where the blood pulse trips
the sun's hooves
over the rooftop
of these cratered acres
and nothing moves.

Little lizard, little lizard
with your eyes sewn open
and your lips stitched tight,
who staked you to your shadow

on the sand?
What carbon visions dripped
to your brainpan
as your pupils widened
and the light
shuddered out?

Gorge on your silence, lizard.
Be bitter, but
be quick about it, since
you can't complain.

    *

Still with me,
lizard? Look:
someone scratched the basalt's
desert varnish, limed
the markings, a map
of their passing, and yours:
an open palm, a spiral,
a star. Someone gouged
a shallow basin, carved
to catch the rain
that never comes, or came
too late for you.

Your death
stains what it touches
a pre-Cambrian ochre
sunset glow.

And now that smutch
is on the corn.
The mothers gather,
the black mouth calls you home.

Listen: cicada:
flute of the ruins.

Shake
the beetle's rattle carapace

and watch
how the clouds come.

      *

O little pinstripe lizard, slit
from groin to chin,
gutted, stuffed with leaves to keep
the magic in,
did no one teach you shun
the sparse
snakebush, its green
too lush for you?

Did no one ever say:
that empty
sky is the sign of plenty, this
is the bowl of the skull,
these are the hands that hold
the eye of the thistle open
and close the doors of the rain?

      *

Listen, lizard.
There was a woman
who appeared
when I was dead inside.
Her tribe climbed
the star-

studded cedar
ladder of the sky,
her hair
fanned out
against the pillow
like the night, her hands
cupped water falling
through my dreams of dry
riverbed and winterkill.

Two of a kind.
You and I, lizard,
we left our skins there.

      *

Little lizard, liquid sibyl,
tap the bitter quill
of forgiveness,
bathe with me in this
abysmal water, lava
font of the dawn.

      *

Little lizard, little lizard
with your eyes sewn open
and your lips stitched tight,
quick! Before they pitch us down
some chimney into hell:

What did you see? What did you say?
What did you threaten to tell?

The Backlook

Now that your ghost has been laid,
now that the beast has been shot,
now that his dam has been spayed
and your daughters who loved you, like, *lots*,
are resettled in Adelaide
(never mind at what cost)
where it's 46 in the shade
and that coat of arms you embossed
on their breasts won't be washed off
with wine or acid or milk,
does your mouth remember the silk
of their skin, and the taste, and the thrill
of their nails raking your face?
Can you still tell them apart
in the dark by their smell, the heat
of the palm pressed to your heart,
taking the Lord's word
without a grain of salt
while you issue the will of the Lord?
Is it as bad as you feared?

No bolt from heaven's vault
you've learned to call the sky?
No *"Whet the blade, my son"*?
No bush combusts in your eyes?

Castaway. Where to?
Vegas? The Poconos?
You'd like to make amends,
but where in hell are your friends?
(Only Dante knows.)
Hell: infected fire:
where the blowfly blows:

it cannot purify
those souls who wish to die:
never consumes what it burns.

You and the voice in your head
take it up in turns.
Are you working the Lord's will?
Does the voice in your head lie still?

Have you chiseled the Decalogue?
Your terror is stuck like a gecko
to the glass your breath won't fog.

Home? A box of night.
Swim in adrenaline
when they screw the roof down tight!

Clay clods rain cold blows
on your soul till your soul's
emptiness echoes.

Now the church bell's tocsin
comes flooding your bloodstream!
What has your life been?
Sin! Sin! Sin! Sin! Sin!

Conjure the garden. Eve—
virginal mien
(*she* won't come again!)
skin freckling in the sun—
maculate satin you peeled
her red scream from,
ripe apple cored,
covenant signed and sealed
kneeling for your Lord?

Wipe the pen, man. You're done.

Anno Domini 1999

I.
I was entering
Rome, and the slash
from Alexandria
swirled through
her outskirts,
the bald heads
of her triumvirs
burned for lime,
your loves, Catullus,
Cavafy, smudging
the shrunk grove
and the queen-
less hive.

The Nile's
fertile green
muck dried
to cake the spine
of an old campaigner,
the felled oak,
this obelisk
rotting on its side.

The sacred
rivers dead
or beheaded,
the old gods,
dust in rut,
the stone
gone, the sun
blind.

Ash
falls like a snow
of salt in the wounds
of the windrows.

*

Romans!
Your new god's flock thins
to a handful
of bystanders and these
armed men who come
to draw down his father
with him
plucked and bloodied and strung
up live
as bait
for the hawk
in a forest
of weeping trees.

*

And what of that tawny
queen whose thighs
ached to encumber
Rome with the Ptolemies'
incestuous offspring,
with the ten plagues
and the twelve tribes?

Her life the stuff
of opera, her aria,
a venomous vein
complaining
in the vulgar tongues:
Coptic, demotic, Italian.

These are her gifts, small
everlastings: river
sickness, cholera, malaria,
the needled mosquito
and the industrious flies.

Isaiah, shall she have
the last word,
penned by the bloody
stings of your scribes?

II.
Through charred sockets, I watch
the torched wasp's nest
of the Colosseum,
blown sands hissing
over hot stones re-echo
the fawn-colored Sibyl's whisper
of the Sirocco, mocking
Cato's immortal
hatred of Dido:
delenda est
Carthago.

The flames of her suicide pyre
lap at the tawny
flank of the Tiber.
His fountain shut,
his green scales drying
duller in the sun,
Sahara is what
the dying Triton
sucks from his
conch-shell horn.

Ovid could say the Black Sea isn't black,
its salt not bitter, his sun-blistered neck
ready to bear the cross-straps of the war-pack
and drudge for Caesar, but he can't come back.

The stumps of Dodona
petrify in the Forum,
the Senate's filibuster drones on.
An iodine wind approximates the sea,
without the relief of the sea.
Lupus est homo homini.

Noon. Out at Fiumicino,
the ceiling falls to zero:

time
shifting its sands
from hand to hand.

In the sun's
air space over Santa
Maria *sopra* Minerva,
a barn owl guts
a pigeon. Keats
weeps. Gibbon
opens his notebook and writes.

Three nuns in dark glasses and wimples
greedily widen their lips
for their *priest stranglers*
drowning in *marinara*.

A wipe. A slow dissolve.
Federico cries *Lights!*
as the room goes and the dark

engulfs what he loves.
Sexless, the vestals cannot strike a spark.

We pay with the faces pressed in our palms for the right
to walk through breathless, expensive halls.
The Renaissance is *In Restauro*—
a classical beauty with her jaw wired shut
points us through the filtered dim where
the state museum puts on display
how Greece and Egypt were raped
repeatedly, easily. Again, the Pope escaped
this hell from Mecca in his summer home.
The sands of the arena seem reserved
for all the stray cats of Rome.

*

Come dusk, the sexual
purr of a solitary
desert leopard
multiplies,

topaz
eyes flashing—
headlamps of Vespas
out prowling the piazzas.

Where is the wolf bitch
who suckled the twins
cast on her breast
in bronze?

Their milky mouths already
rounding the O
of *Omertà*, it's a silence
they imbibe.

Her scalding, black milk jets
into our speechless, lean-
lipped mouths from the she-wolf's teats
of an espresso machine.

       *

A live bee sips
at a chiselled calyx
in a cemetery waiting
for rain.
The lockjaw wrought-
iron gates rusted
shut, a mossy silence cropping the carved
Etruscan legend running the length of the lintel:

Fummo come voi. Sarete come noi.

Honeycombed
marble sarcophagi
of the Popes' tombs,
(excellent cadavers!)
and these dead,
anonymous because
they refuse to give
even their own names.

I, whose mother's
patronym is Caia,
from which I derive
to fall, to fall silent,
am startled by
the throbbing of the hive.

We were like you.
You will be like us.

The same. The same
death corrects
our indiscretions.

Clapperless, the swung
bell does justice
to us who when
called upon to witness,
swallow our tongues.
Come. Stand
under the shade
of this tower—
an inverted well,
a poured-out cauldron
scalding the faithful,
this iron-age
flower, that hangs
by a tendril,
with its petals in heaven
and its root in hell—

until the nib of this pen split
like the tail of the scarab's shell
and a drop distilled from the night
rolls onto the page.

III.
The best that I wrote was only a paraphrase
of the light that exacts compassion for these dead.
Look, Isaiah, the *Rainbow! Redemption. Revenge.*
As if the Biblical prophets had pirated
the names of ships from my tongue's imperial days.

Inheritance

The Parthenon—
cloud-white
marble temple.
Quarried sky.

Perfection.

Does it always come down to
north against south?
Salt tang of dialect,
lemons and capers, versus
the long-necked
blonde with the delicate mouth?

Sea-born, yes.
But even Botticelli's
Venus was always
more gold than foam.

And the over-made-up
Neapolitan whore
busted trolling the wharves
in bedclothes in daylight is pure
Athenian polychrome.

At this end
of the iron age,
ushering in a millennium
of plutonium and lead,
rub the slate
clean. When laurel-leaved
brows bend to their hemlock

without protest, remember
this transported girl,
more faithful than Atlas,
this caryatid, trapped
in the steel cage
of her scaffolding, dancing
with all the weight
of heaven on her head.

The Climb

"Arrived?" he asked in surprise. "What does that mean?"
"I know. It means: now we are leaving."
                        —Kazantzakis, *Report to Greco*

Don't say it's inevitable. Nothing's inevitable,
except the heat of this thirsty siesta you'll never escape,
rust flaking from a lacework balcony rail
to the throb of a diesel tender crossing the harbor,
her face on the pillow, eyes closed, almost asleep,
while your heart keeps pumping it out and taking it in,
the Cupid's bow of her lip caked white with dust
from the dry clay roads, the resinous
fresh-cut smell of pine rising, and gasoline
spilled to the ditches in—
but the city itself is immaterial,
since noon's amnesia will sweep the approaches clean.
Call it Thebes for convenience, let the blind speak, the blade wait
on its sheaf of immaculate straw.
The sunswept steps to the scaffold stay hot
under your bare feet. Nikos,
why not lift a hand to prevent this?
You've been down all the roads,
Spain, Sicily, Greece,
they lead to a single place—
a broad plaza whose salt cobbles blaze.
The chorus is bored, but the face
of the man on the dais matches the bills
that prop him in place.
If the speaker drags out the dead,
the sun will not pause in its crossing, no one object,
least of all these familiar faces whose silence will say
your heartbeat is treason.

She lies asleep on the bed.

So where is the hope that daybreak promised,
lost or misplaced—it takes up less space
than a seed or pinch of dirt in a pant-cuff,
and the faith that if it dies in the sun
it will fatten like grass in the rain?

Wake up! You must have been dreaming, Nikos,
they've metered the rain,
nothing is green here except the fatigues
of the leader towering over the podium,
behind him, his generals dressed in the same
khaki as the toads. The police are conducting
a door-to-door search. There's nothing
they can take from you, there's nothing you own.
But they envy the poverty your love gives you, Nikos.

The black sun of the loudspeaker's bellmouth has called
your name, the plaza contracts with the last of its shadows
to a raw box whose nailheads, dressed with crosses, scald.

The four corners of the world
touch the edge of this coffin.

Quick! Knock wood, Nikos! Run!

Last night in the *taverna*
(unseen for how many years?)
waggling his chin in a way
inherited from his grandfather,
looking up biting his thread:
"Nikos!"
And was it really Stavros,
removing his glasses, wiping the tears
from the frame, letting the cloth
fall getting

to his feet but gingerly setting
thimble and needle and thread
on a plate to embrace you, then spreading
his hands in a gesture that took everything in,
Stavros, shaking his head:
"Why did you come back, Nikos?
To bury the dead?"

How can you tell him
they never stay buried for good?
And how light they travel!
Wherever you go, you find your dead
awaiting your arrival.
Thirty centuries
haunted by Helen's face.
All the old battles still being fought,
living out of a suitcase.

That was last night.
In this room, this cube of light,
your answer, Nikos, echoes.

Now as she turns on her side,
wavelets break over her nape.

You want her so bad you can taste
the salt sheen on her skin
just by looking. Christ!

Who the conqueror, who
the sacrifice? Minerva swerves
homeward from Rome.

Her bright curls pour
over the stoney

coastline at Aulis.

The D.T.'s

> ... *the car broke down, and an arrow*
> *of blood on a boulder pointed*
> *the way to Aleppo.*
>   —Eugenio Montale, "Syria"

Global warming? It's the dogdays, Eugenio. Ratchet the heat!
We've closed down the Colosseum—can't sell a seat
with white cops offing black teens for free in the street.

National Pork Board stuffs House caucus? Sweet!
Play chicken with the Senate (the other white meat)
on cruise control. Rock the Swamp! Swipe right. Swipe left. Repeat.

Jack a Hamilton strapped, do two-to-four.
Pay tax on millions? What's the bottom 99 percent for?
(*Trickle-down*'s pigeon for *piss-on-the-poor*.)

Money doesn't talk, it purrs: *too small to save, too big to fail.*
The Huckster-in-Chief himself is up for sale:
our one-and-only second chance at the third rail!

Perjury trap! Witch hunt! Our democracy's cursed.
What Swamp Thing starts to life now her waters have burst?
Kool-Aid, Prez? *Citizens Benighted! Roberts' rules! You first!*

Which of us hasn't led a blameless life?
We're hacking and frac'ing and vac'ing and liking our life
on Facebook, we follow on Twitter, we Kindle and Tinder the wife.

I am a saint for sinning, the bishop of hippos
wallowing in it, killing the competition—lighting them up with
   my Zippo,
I find your arrow of blood on a boulder pointing the way to Aleppo.

Go, little soul, my body's host and guest.
The globe is bleeding refugees, the West
is stitching Kevlar to its Sunday best.

III

Petra

for Lavinia Currier

My laughter
is the crackle
of kindling

at midnight, the moon,
my white goat caught
on a thorn.

You are a man on his knees
peeking through a keyhole
when the door is open. Heaven

is my tent-roof
hung by a rope from the sky.
Sleep with me,

I am sweet tea, I am these
red seeds
on a white plate.

Don't let your heart
be a bird that starves
with food in its cage!

Aubade

A month apart,
seven hours talking, then
you slept for an hour in my arms.

Dawn, and the death-fugue
of car alarms—
the music you woke to,
our urban aubade.

You dressed. The clock
would not stop

peeking through its hands
as you stood
on the cold parquets, bare
except for your stockings
and collared top,
composing the morning
around you,
brushing your hair.

Suddenly, tail in the air,
you were my
tan-thighed Diana
hunting among
the thrown-off bedclothes
for your slingshot thong.

Your hand found my hand,
but not for long.

*

Hush of tires
on blacktop. Pulling away,
your face through the tinted
window of a cab.

Then, between scab-
colored brick
buildings, an inch
of blue, and beneath it,
smudging the dusk, the Hudson
burned like a highway flare.

Reflected sunrise:
smear of blood
on a glass slide
under the lens
of the instant,
unfocused, but magnified.

*

Bored, the sun
tortured me with blades
of light through the blind,
with your dime-store hairpin
glowing like tungsten,
like your eyes, looking up
startled from sleep,
your scent on the linen,
the red of your lips
left on a winecup.

Neither of us said "I love you,"
neither of us cried.

Everything we say
will be swallowed by silence.

My silence lied.

Vespers

Languorous grass
in a watercourse;

the poppy bud
and the open flower,

their silk,
satin, and suede;

you are sunfire stored
in a golden pear;

the hour of forgiveness;
hour of the star;

asleep, you are
wheat,

the full moon laid
in swales on the bedsheet

by the blades of the blind;
you are wind

unbraiding the black
manes of waves;

you are smoke
rising from incense;

clear sapphire;
the pale blue flame

of the rosemary;
you are reeds, the ache

and suck of the sea;
you are wine fermenting,

the alchemy
by which grapes change

into tears and dreams;
you are steam

from tea, and the future's
unreadable leaves;

you are the sands
of the crossroads; my salt

hay and driftwood
bonfire, quick

to kindle, slow
to blaze;

you are water raised
to parched lips

from a well,
each breast a handful;

you are dusk, and the whispered
vespers of bees.

Can't Anyone Untie Us?

Stars & spurs & Spain,
and she wants a bed off the floor!
I—I want more.
High tablelands of wheat.
Days as gold as grain.
Iruña. San Fermín.
Bulling our way south
through the feral heat.
More raw dawns, her mouth
that rained-on roof tile red;
more sunlight scythed and baled
and, scratchy, stacked in the shed;
more thirst; more tempest; more
hunger that multiplies
the risen loaves of the road stones
by the vanishing points of her eyes,
the heart's devastations
over an empty chair
worse than the breaking of nations,
the torch nailed up by its hair
to the acid light that scours
the threshing floor of the mind
in Goya's black hours
where he caught my kind;
more brushwork that turns with the swirl
of a *muleta* between
the nights when the rats are here
nibbling the foam mattress
like cheese, and Everclear
keeping the lamps lit
with a cool, blue flame.
What's wrong with a bed on the floor?
I paint your name in salt
and oxblood on the door.

Ice

Eye of the thistle,
frozen open. Rice

grass. Winterfat
thins to a whisper.

Bare volts crackle
in the hair of the tamarack.

Each stone grips
a star in its fist.

The life I loved
didn't love me back.

Truro / Angers, Anjou

The wines of Angers, too volatile to travel—
like Hecuba on horseback
who rocks to sleep and dreams she spreads her knees
to give birth to a torch.
                        Duned bluff.
Dragonfly fetched up on compass grass.
Half wind backing through the prickly wind rose.
Hissing gas lamp. Sizzling grasses, sands.
Children's voices blowing through the rooms.
One step behind you, beyond you,
slate bay rain
                blurs and erases.
                              Starboard lights
wobble in a saucer. Fireflies. Faces
rippling behind window glass.
Green wings in the lilac dusk.
When did you become everything I wanted?
The stars are hardly farther than your hand—
spark of dark garnet, three gold bands.
Angers is someplace else,
skin like silk on clavicle and pulse—
first time I've seen you in fifteen years,
if my palm touched your face I'd scorch.

Morpho

The sun's been cut and beaten till bare sky
shows through its goldfoil—daylight
weighs less than it did in the heat of August.
Green gold not white gold suits you best. July
was green gold. The grain of August is the yellow
of King Croesus. This month is Midas, white-
faced, hiding in the panic grasses.
The cedar still casts shadows, but none so plush
that we could drink from. Remember the embers smouldering
in the garden? This season plays charades.
Her paper roses are all wear and tear.
We feign guessing, though we know what's missing.
Slyer, the lilac unpinning the heart from its sleeve.
Ephemeral? Think of the honey bee, queen

for a day, ebony on gold on jet—
you on velvet in your box at the ballet—
except for the ruby *bindi* on her belly
(Downton Abbey redubbed in New Delhi).
No pinched monarch barely bending the stem
she rests on, she clothes her workers in fur,
yet it means death if they get it wet.
Carcanet discarded for the day at Yale,
prepping in bedclothes, gunning the Hudson, my duckie,
the usual doom of drakes hard on your heels,
high on gas fumes and adrenaline,
grading papers, plumage drooping, before noon's
genius lunch, high tea with a tycoon,
teaching in a sheath of liquid metal

under your favorite raincoat from McQueen—
high on teen hormones and the sense of sin
that goes with innocence, easy in your skin
but not immune (undone by love), undine,
pinchbeck bangles jangling at the chalkboard,
writing circles around your students (writing
circles round us all)—*How do we know
what we know?* —
martyred in Blahniks, the assassin's gold stiletto.
The surf still hisses like fat in the pan but the sands
aren't turning to glass underfoot as when you walked here,
mermaid, selkie, your bare feet bleeding
in meter down the page. *Coup de foudre!*
Love, blind? I saw you, I saw I'd trade

my soul for a kiss.
My beauty-spotted beauty, my minx of Minsk,
which is the element you'll be returning
to? Changeling, gosling, Goosegirl, your goblet's
lost for good. Shocking? Girl, if you're thirsty,
touch your tongue to the current or drink with your hands.
I'm drowning in air without you, water
so cold it's burning the topo maps of your contours
off my fingertips. *Do you miss me?*
I knew riches when you skinned me with a look
—green flash to rival last summer's blue
kingfisher sipping from your willow ware.
You knit your poems from nothing: river mist,
racetrack bloodlines, bits of rickrack, matchbooks,

signs—neon not supernatural.
I miss that and Miss This: uncanny
tales of your two familiars and their kittens.
Bella Donna, you are wide-eyed, shaking
me awake: *How do you want to die?*
Swear, Mab? Keep my answer under
your foxfur hat? You read me like a book.
Must I lie in the field full of folk,
shirty in the shrunk cuffs of my *hic jacet*?
Poor morpho, *your* jacket's in tatters—or is that
the sky shedding its skin over Manhattan,
waiting for the Götterdämmerung to begin?
—I want your breath on me, my hand in your mouth—
butterfly brushing the touchpad as I write this.

Chez Nous

A-frame, palace, Athens, Georgia, Mars,
Cheapside pub-snug or Cow Hollow's salty bars,
gypsy wagon, siren's island, one or two
staterooms with the outside passage view,
mud and wattle hut, or yurt
with a front yard of swept dirt
and a camel (what a flirt!)—
that *dromedary*, Darling, will not do!
(I think he really has a thing for you.)

Redwood hot tub in Missoula,
the back room behind Miss Lula,
San Francisco, the Big Easy,
Park Ave or *slightly* sleazy,
under dreamsmoke on a junk,
in the stone cell of a monk,
sett, pad, den, dam, dive,
a Petri dish, a lily pad, a hive,
mermaid grotto (when we're blotto)
or the Taj we won at Lotto—
anything's OK if I'm with you.
I don't mind the White House if you're blue,
or the Cardinal's (all in scarlet)
with the Pope's own German *var*let
and a barman and a maid to wait on you.
If we're pressed I guess a wooden shoe would do.

At the gate in Hialeah
aw the pahty in the reah
down to Ivy's (nevah see hah)
aw some clammy bathyspheah,
in a cloakroom full of hats,

on the altar at St. Pat's,
in a nutshell (filbert, almond, or cashew)—
to be bunged up for a month alone with you!

Cherry orchard where we're tortured by the view?
Dacha, brownstone, kiva, temple, dollhouse, pile,
felucca sailing down a reach of the Blue Nile,
magic mountain, public fountain,
five-star hotel (but who's countin'?),
Lady Chapel, May Day bower,
house of cards, a high-rise tower,
pirate's lair, the Suez locks,
or a Pontiac on blocks,
the cat's cradle of a tipsy sailor's yarn,
a love nest in a hayloft in a barn—
Sweetheart, it is really up to you—
a willow cabin or a tent would do:
Home is anyplace my heart lies down with you.

Crowes Pasture

The salt marsh by the abandoned fish weir's
sunk boards at Quivet, wood silvered by a century's
muds and tides: the sky is iron, rusting
round the edges; ravens settle like scorched
pages in the oak. Cordgrass, couch grass,
foxtail, poverty, teasel, needle-and-thread—
wind hissing frigid through forsaken acres—
each night Orion nocks an arrow to the bowstring,
Bear's gutshot blood burns bright in hips and haws.
White-hot talons of a dark-phase hawk
dive where tomorrow's blue moon has to rise.
Salt hay between the treeline and the ebbline—
lap robe fallen from the starry hay wain
deepening wheelruts past the hunters' bowers—
elkskin pulled tight to the throats of rushes,
burnt umber in the wet, flat flanks; dulled gold
spine-tufts that stand up rising, falling
to ocean's onslaught twice a day from solstice
to solstice; amethyst dimming in the smoky lamps—
sea lavender's branching candelabra—
the temperature drops ten degrees in twenty minutes,
glasswort frosted, brittle underfoot,
all fall its scarlet kept throbbing through the fog.
Windgusts strumming dunegrass are the rippling
muscles of a lion running under
the wind; nothing for it but
over the top into the brunt, cast sand
rasping skin off my lids: hoodwinked, blindfold,
blooded on your stuff of silk and lace:
I could nose my way past Gloucester back to Dover
and find you in the dark with my bare hands.
I bend my neck and lean against the beach

blowing down the beach to Brewster, whitecaps
cracking me up—sideways waves
no longer water, not yet ice—
there, thrown on the sand, a torpedo fish,
ray-round, brick thick, snot brown, barbless, devil
tail with caudal fin (from this
to your Thane of Cawdor, a short hop
as the crow flies over Crowes)—a marvel
the gulls have already started in on, eyes
as always first to go. All's fair, Dan Cupid
or his blind old sea dog
come frisking to his whistle like a pup—
I don't know what I have in my hands.
Of course I have to lift the damn thing up—
bottom blanched white, a sucked cut, rose
feathering edges of the underdisc.
Step on one alive, 200 volts—
(hoodman blind played naked among the sea stones)—
each volt a tiny tooth from the dolphin's livewire
smile I saw last summer, close up and strung,
each one a fallen star, echo
of an explosion, faceted sapphire
anklet of electricity—
as when my hand closed round your ankle, taking charge,
the thrill of that first time still going through me—
now there's no going back or letting go—
the waves have worked their way around behind me—
that knot tied, shocking beauty.

IV

Winterreise

As the body ages,
does your spirit grow younger?
My spirit cries and rages.
Satisfaction? Too little too late.
Kissing the maid at the mill,
enough's *never* enough.
I want what feeds the *hunger*.
To be sated is
to suck tart greengages.
Going going gone.
All my pretty ones?
Songs of Love and Hate
or songs of love and loss?
Shall we play
Schubert or Leonard Cohen?
Airbnb the *Schloss*
or crash outside the gate?
What do you want from me?
Tonight should I be
Macheath or Macduff?
Shall I lick the blade
or weep into my cuff?
My spirit cries and rages.
The body loves its cages.
The spirit likes sleeping rough.

Ocean

My blue-lipped, unsubtle mother, this summer sea
wants me stretched out naked on her bed.
Her glib tongue's numbed my pulses. Soothingly,
her kisses cooled the bruises on my head:

fontanelle and temple, ear and eye
ceding their fever to the spray's plump lips.
Her grey flesh begs my health and youth to die.
Cold grease, her kisses smeared along my lips.

Yet her waters washed away the mortal stain
of childhood's wishing to remain a child.
Sad fats and acids ate into my brain.
I saw where the dogfish keeps his white bones piled.

I saw a mare's nest float on the ocean, wild
stallions ramp to mount each swaybacked wave.
Horseshoe-crab-tail trocars rasped and filed
my neck free of her torc. The salt-walled cave-

mouth gripped and gaped behind my murdered head.
Crisp sea-foam laced a skullcap round my crown.
No Queen of Egypt fished me into bed.
I was Moses, I dozed and floated, only face down.

I held my breath and did the dead man's float,
eyes closed, my lashes fanned by gill and fin.
On the third day I began to bloat
till not a wrinkle marred my silvered skin.

Stiff fiddlers picked stitches from that too-tight coat,
my eyelids jimmied open by the blue
crab claws unknotting fascia from nerve tissue.
The pigfish dribbled flesh. I heard the shoat

grunt his hunger. Gold and silver coins
hissed on the waters. What I saw was scales
falling from the mermaid's dragon tail.
I dipped there where the human woman joins

the salty furrow closing round my cries.
I was her husband. She was no one's wife.
Her broad flukes stirred the waters into life.
Her sequins pressed pale half-moons in my thighs.

No. Three weeks I drifted while our banns were read
to the bell buoy's hammering Angelus.
Calm nights the stars fell. They lay like spread
petals on the waters over us.

No. Calm nights the stars fell. They lay like bread
upon the water till the dawn wind blew
the seabirds ravening after them, and drew
the plumes of whitecaps crashing on my head.

Waves smashed Atlantis back to pink-grained sand.
The moon is both a grinding wheel and knife.
But we were lovers in a former life!
I held her crescent scepter in my hand.

African Funeral, Anjou

*Matchflames in the cattails, mating redthroats set
the meadow smoking through thatched straw and fog.*

Gashed embers, crèche of feathers, death-
bed hush and wish, rushlight
guttering on the threshold,

rustler of dovecotes, kestrel, Abakuá
seer, Dida king
in your tie-dyed raffia
suit of autumnal colors (cinnamon,
clove, gold), your black-magic
witch-doctor leopardskin
vest and gorget,

roadkill hawk, hooked
beak smashed flatter than an arrowhead
on the macadam of the allée below
the river and a row
of plane trees standing guard
in Maghreb desert camo,
your crushed skull,
that egg, that *O*, that zero
where nothing said what it meant
through my open mouth:
death's open eye.

Tetragrammaton

His horse is scorpion and his prose
is buried in the dresser
under keys and coins and clothes.
Who is his lover? Who is his confessor?
Ask the waves. Ask the sheaves. Ask the winds.
Ask the darkness between stars.
His pride brightens daybreak and his sins
are written on the petals of the rose.

Light is whose seed? Glaciers
calve in whose wake? Who chummed
blood from the ocean, stitched it veins,
and set the tiger pacing in its cell,
made ant a dragon in a world of grains?
His presence is splendor, his absence
deafens hell. And since
the arc of the stallion's neck
is the sign of his triumph,
grass is his mercy, dew
shines his magnificence.
His lowliest creatures go
clothed in the rainbow, the great
are scaled or skinned
alive to please him.
Look how his anger makes
the peacock watch its back, his laughter chills
the rain that imitates it. Silence is
the last and greatest of his canticles.

How Quietly, How Quickly

I pass the churchyard's kissing gate, the paved
walkway to the stone stile and the grave-
yard, pass hillside vaults
where winter's dead wait while the grounds crew salts
the roads and limes their bodies
and a south wind thaws
the soil the sexton's pickaxe claws
the roof off—watch him
move on from this dugout once he trusts
his shovelers to blade it deep into
transit camp and relocation hub
under the star
chambers of the beetle and the grub,
there where the worm works, making castings
of anatomies in the blast
furnace of the August sun
when the russet fox outruns
the dog days. Pass
the locust's brittle chrysalis, the glass
castles of cicadas' skeletons,
study that patch
of couch grass grown rife
over pauper graves and Indian graves where no
headstones remember the names
entered in death's manifest, the owl's *Who's Who*,
pause here a moment, climb
past these ghosts: the pikes
of foxglove, the spike-studded mace
sweetgum's wielding in a narrow place,
cut between barberry hedges,
enter on the sly

a tree-lined avenue
where the named and wealthy dead till Judgment Day
reside in shade
thrown by porphyry follies, obelisks:
tombs with a view.

The path descends again. I thread my way
between blackened monuments
acid rain has stained and honeycombed
white marble Bibles, cherubs, lambs that hold
the place of children lost in infancy,
those whom death
measled with fevers, those who drowned
as white-capped waves of flu crashed on the wards.
Here snow drifts over them, apple blossom foams
above them in the garden close
making visible the wind
that's stirring it, I see
how quietly, how quickly moss
will sponge the uncials from my slate, time squeeze
life's sweetness out between
the cupped palms of paired years' parentheses.

Better to feel
every gust that blows
than none at all, like those
who have gone before.

Gone where? Rot
into the earth, or burn
and loft to drift
in ashes on the air?
Bury me high—
a scaffold in a tree to feed
the raptors.

Which closing year is mine?
I was here in March. Bare maples held
sheets of steel up for the sun to weld.
Now willows scribbling in the dirt decline
to give me any sign.

Leave me time to reap the crop
I planted when I set
out ploughing verses with a pen,
this nib my share in the earth—

catch the salt wind in a net
of words, close haul white
sails beating seaward, spanked with light
(incandescence of a moth in flight);
distill the scent
of hay in lady's bedstraw, blazingstar
marking the trail from me to where you are
my queen, my queen, whom monarchs come to woo
on stained glass wings,
and painted ladies trimmed in sable, too,
duenna'd by the moon, in whose train come
gypsy stitchers, hump-backed munchers, twelve-
eyed, nearly blind from making lacework
of a maple leaf—or is that din armies
marching into grief? The mingling
of our breath, however brief.

Space however curt to gather in
spate of rain at midnight on the skin,
key turning in the wards of a locked door,
shadow play of firelight on the floor;
skim voices off the crystal set of twin
wine glasses on a table;
coin silver, quarry moonlight from the mirror;
cast autumn's shock troops, redcoats, falling

on Boston Common, on avenue and street;
the mingling of our breath, however fleet.

By such small steps time
brings us to our height
of glory, jacks us up
to fall. While
we rise, time
cuts its teeth on us,
pins us by those cogs to our shadow.

Time is our error,
we cannot set it right;
our defeat's inevitable
despite our feints, our flight.
And yet. And yet, we'd have
one more joyous night.

Time, oh times, you danced me
out of moods, or wept, or whipped
me into one. Love was a bloodsport—
Catherine wheel of sparks
and stars and torn
petals arcing
onto the mahogany
cobbles of the court;
the blending of our breath,
however short.

They say time banks the fire and brings
a calm to many things?

If I could sleep I'd sleep
with my hands in the fire
of your hair.

Let it end like this,
my mortal portion
of love and terror:

cavalry charging through the crowded square,
Peterloo, Petersburg, Portland, anywhere,
Plaza de Armas, Plaza Athénée,
or that gem from the string of stone
pensions studding the Biscay shore
from Pointe de Pern to Cabo Finisterre.
I've come back to find you

—although I swore I wouldn't—
sitting on the bed,
in your lap an awn
of wheat, staring out
the French doors open
to the balcony:
all is lost

to a dusk as sheer
as your nightshirt,
soft as your cheek I reach
to touch against
my will—*Cuidado,
cara!*—remember?—

if you tilt your head
your face catches
the last light off the bay,
sure as your hands rise,
your eyes say everything
you never wanted to say
while you slowly draw
the gold pin from your hair
so night can follow day—

and take my breath away—

Metamorphosis

If I've been rough-
handed with my life,
who knows what silk
may yet be made of me?

Let my reeds green again,
sedges feather
star-tipped under
a celestial dew.

Grant me a hand
in the great mystery,
holy roller
scarab shoving
my dungball sun
under the infinite
arch of sky
I'll navigate
by the Milky Way
that all might fructify.
Or may I be
a pismire-participant
in the dark art
of myrmecochory—ant
dispersal of seeds.

Every sentence I write
ends in a period. Or
exclamation point!
Or question mark, right?
Those ink dots common
to all three—same size
as the eggs you lay,
Bombyx mori-

turi te
salutamus—

soft-mouth
silk moth, we

who are about to
die salute you.

Bombyx, bind me
as a pupa to your truth,

teach me faith in
my fifth instar,

my Phoenix-exit
into something
strange.

*

And you, shadowy one,
leaning into the light, hurtling
from the future
to our meeting
on the page,
set this book down
partway open
on the fore-edges
of its boards,
spine the ridgeline
of my A-frame
paperwasp enclave, this
tent of words.

Spin my lines out
to a tensile filament,

speak them into a
tissue of sound.

This is my chrysalis, my
papyrus cocoon:

gauze dipped
in the heart's salts—

like the mantle
of a hurricane lamp,

shall I blaze and consume myself
with the dark I include?

    *

I used to tell the toughs
among my Waltham friends
*See you in Hell or Haverhill
before this night ends.*

That day comes closer when
whatever death is mine
starts showing and is
brought full term.

I've been rough-
handed with my life, torching
draft after draft of it
for light to write you by.

Caught in the halo
of that follow spot,
dancer on the edge
of existence and non-existence,
all the alchemy has to be yours.

You're the mage: Merlin-
falcon, king-maker, sage.

I'm the volunteer
assistant tripping
on the steps to the stage.

Paging through these
poems, reader, gentling
my blood with your touch, don't
close the book on me,
turn its leaves
mulberry—feast
for the silkmaker worm.

Waking

shaken from a dream of youth, whose
lost love goes
barefoot on hottop, through brambles, clothes
her beauty in the wreckage of the rose.

V

For Johnny

As mourners keep
    Let us pray
arriving graveside,
the priest begins the rites,
scanning faces
for a look that
    Eternal rest grant
promises response.

I study the buttons on my cuff, the way
green reeds scrape the sky into the lake.
My mind is aloft with the hawk
hunting out of the sun,
my body burns to cross
that water a gust has swept and creased.
    Does anyone have any
    words he'd like to say?
"Black is the beauty of the brightest day."
"The baily berith the bell away"
bubble up to my lips.
I bite my tongue, and let
showy roses gnaw their raw wood stake.
One budmouth bobs up on a flaw
of wind to hiss: *Press*
your thumb tip
to a thorn, and think
of nothing. Nothing
clarifies like pain
drawn to a needle-fine
locus in the brain.

What it said, I did. I'd seen
your widow enter church. She touched
two fingers to their reflection on the font's
coppery water, blessed herself, and walked
the nave like one who sleepwalked in
the aftermath of gleaners,
as if her hem brushed dew
from grassheads leveled by the scythe,
her skirts heavy with it, and her progress
hushed by what she burnished,
passing through.
Narcotic walk—no, not that—
a convalescent
tenderness—she held
her body off as if
it hurt to touch the earth.
She reached the chancel, raised
her palm to her bosom,
pressed it to your casket's
blue metallic lid above
your hands crossed on your heart.
Watched Deacon bless
your body in its coffin, drape
the pall. Genuflected then, half
curtsy, still
the Southern belle she was
when she conquered you
along with Property and Torts
first term at Georgetown Law.
As she stood, she raised
her face to the Holy Spirit—
stone wings
straining for liftoff
from the top of the altar screen.

Beneath the veil, her hair,
not braided loosely in a rope and pinned
above her nape, as usual, but spread
like goldleaf across her shoulders, like the sheaf
of barley on jet cloth at harvest home.
She turned to step into the pew. I caught
clearly for a second
whatever grief her mouth knew,
lipstick fixed. Her eyes were the sunrise
on a swath of death as wanton
as the cuts on the stubble fields
from Shiloh through Gettysburg to Appomattox.

My knees gave, seeing that, believing you
could see it, too.

You once told me she
was the only being you
adored. She honored you
and your last wish. Last night
at your wake, I knelt and said
a Paternoster and
Angelus at your casket.
She sent you out
girded for battle, feet
cleated, favorite
war club within reach:
she buried you
with your three iron
in those bespoke Treccani
two-tone stingray golf shoes.

*

Returning from
your second tour of duty in Vietnam,
out from under command
with your back to the wall,
you sent me four
postcards from Bangkok, six
from Luzon, rocking out, awash
in the offing, awaiting transport:

> "Every millisecond of life's
> a judgment call.
> Yet soon, very soon, we'll have
> no more choice at all."

> "So, then? Troop among crows
> in universal sacerdotal black, or choose
> Jezebel's and the cardinal's scarlet,
> red as seconal?"

> "At the outset of the French-
> Indochina war, who owned the most
> land in Vietnam? And at the end?
> Best shot? Ho Chi *Minh*?"

> "A trifle wide, my friend.
> Correct for wind
> and the curve of the earth:
> the *Vati*can."

> "Christ! *Render unto Caesar*
> *what is Caesar's.*
> Win church, win state:
> *Roma Victrix.*"

> "The scales of justice
> ponder and equivocate

    until some new
    balance point is found."

    "Have we learned nothing since
    Dante conscripted Florence
    to populate Inferno's
    electron shells,"

    "Emperor and Pope,
    Ghibbeline and Guelph
    contending still?
    Myself?"

    "Give me Kit
    Marlowe every time:
    Why, this is hell,
    nor am I out of it."

    "There's this one thing happened.
    Thing I did. When I
    ~~severed~~ served as a
    LURP I can't erase."

And a letter later from the States:

    "Five nights outside our lines,
    the last of my team left alive,
    humping my carcass back
    south to Song Ve to be debriefed,
    I come on this . . .
    if the crossroads where two footpaths intersect
    beside a paddy is a village, then a village.
    Torched hooches smoke and reek
    like smudgepots in an orange grove back home.
    Not a dog barks. No buffalo
    chewing things over under a yoke

off in the shade. My next step
guns the chainsaw drone of flies.

Shot from such close range that I can smell
the powder burns before I even see them,
half-naked bodies piled in two slick stacks.
Heap of singed tire-tread
sandals, clothes—more ash
than fabric, held together by
stink of burnt rubber under
the cleansing benediction
of gasoline.

Whose work was this?
Ours or theirs? I stoop to check
the shells. Someone's picked
the spent brass up—bad sign:
definitely not army
SOP. The Company? I mull
that. A leaf
shifts, puff
of dust off rice straw,
middle distance lofts the glint
of sun on metal through elephant grass down trail
before my feet detect the footfalls that even now
are coming for me down
the hallway to my kip here in D.C.,
the listening post between
my ears grabs laughter—
they haven't spotted me.

No time to hide & nowhere
if there was time.
Slip into the paddy, I'd have to cross
their sightline, field of fire.

Next assessment
happens in a synapse when my life
expectancy is shorter than the breath
it takes to say it:
only way out is in—

among the bodies. The one
below me's warm. Left hand scuttles
quick as a paddy crab to stop the cry
will kill us both. Voices
focus to close-up. Breath held:
a revolver's
cylinder spins.
Hammer-click—
all but piss myself—
of a *Zippo!*: flint-
rasp; inhalation.
Echo-click: Zippo
shut with a flick of the wrist.

New voices, one
clearly in command. They move
a long way off. Two
drift back. Fade to bug-hum. Null
now. Night
cold surges up from the muddy
thighs of mother earth, not *mine*—
what would *she* be doing
bathing in moonlight on the Plain of Reeds?
Hours I cleave
tight to him—to suck
the last warmth from his body
into mine, and so survive? So end
his pain? Or pour
mine into him, fire him up, and so
snuff both? *Save* both?

Tripping on fear's acid
IV drip, not a thought
I do not burn through this night
long enough for every maggot
whim to worm new
pathways through the grey
labyrinth behind my eyes
until I know—just *know*:
the bamboo-shadow-clad
platoon—dispersed like mist.
I do not want to see
his visage, who
twins me in this womb.
My arm's gone
pins and needles, left leg
numb. Belly-
elbow wriggle-crawl
out of my cocoon—
teeth welded to my hand.
Jolt free, his head
snaps back, brow to chin
floodlit by the moon. Landscape
flows, leaves strobe in motion—
I'm on my knees and leaning
over the black mirror
of paddy water,
kneecap slips, hand
plunges in the drink—
shatters my reflection swimming
away from me in ripples, slivers
of glass and silver
elvers as the cold light of daybreak broke me
loose.
       I woke
alone. Bodies gone. G.I.
hypodermic in my arm.

Why not just waste me?
Did someone pump
truth serum in, cull the bloodsticks
of my secrets from me?

Spooks. Who else?
Top brass? VC?
Lord of the Dead?
Hades, is it?
Aka Lucifer? Pluto? Dis?

Have you tried
to hide from Hades?
That night I took
the jump knife
strapped to my calf, jimmied
open a place
far inside myself—
there Hades lay in wait.

The thing I can't erase—
I wouldn't put it to you if I had
anyone else to ask.

He had my face.

Does that mean I have none?

Or I have his?"

*

We spoke last
a week after treatment when a better
rehab bed was found:

    "*Might* have been agent orange—"

'Meaning the V.A.—'

    "Not likely. Berenice is hot to sue."

'Let her! She's smart enough to whup 'em!—
Justice herself, balance in one hand,
sword in t'other—
Not to bring peace, but a—Not bad
as the motto on her business card, except
someone else owns the brand. Give 'em hell
but build your strength first, bro. Chill.
Important thing is, you're going to get
entirely well. Why, *the very
hairs on your head are*—'

    "Gone. Right before chemo.
    Sawbones said it would fall out anyway.
    Shaved *everything*. You want to know from chill?
    Slightest breeze, I'm freezing. Must've got
    the Barber from Brazil."

'Remember that big blow on the Solimões?'

    "Rio Negro, bro. *You*
    were scared our boat was going to tip!"

'A modicum of caution.
How wide's the river there, outside Manaus?'

    "Twenty-two miles across."

'And a mile straight down to the bottom.'

    "In *that* current? Nothing goes straight down."

'How far, confluence to source?'

> "You want to reach the remotest stone age tribes
> they say you have to paddle fifty
> centuries upriver."

'Almost as long as we kept revising—'

> *"amending"*—

'our list ranking
the places we'd been—'

> "the many we dreamed of seeing—"

'the few we'd go back to.'

> "Venice."

'Vientiane.'

> "Not my list—"

'Lake Turkana.'

> "Mongolia. Kazakh golden
> eagle festival—"

'Tops them all! Lightning round?'

> "Worst bite you ever?"

'Or sip. Fall River rules. No hand—'

> "sanitizer highballs."

'Croc po'boy, hold the roll.'

> "Kumiss. Fermenting
> while you ride the mare."

'Cat-poop coffee.'

> "Hoss-spittle coffee."

'Haggis.'

> "Spider fritters."

'Grubs. See under *raw*.'

> "Maasai blood milkshake."

'Hot or cold?'

> "Hot and frothy. Not the taste. The thought."

'Nightcrawlers—crawling off the plate.'

> "Fugu."

'Puffer sushi? The Russian roulette fish?
Supposed to be ambrosia.'

> "When you're *already* a god. Turned to metal in *my* mouth."

'Eating your own death, if the knife slipped.'

> "Eating your fear. Adrenaline.
> Once the poison hits,
> in the sweaty minutes you've got left,
> how do you skype your wife and tell her
> she married a fool?"

'At the buzzer!
Undefeated! One more round?'

    "Martin, not for me, or you, the smooth
    casket lacquered like a bento box.
    Yours will be knotholed, wormwood, rough-hewn,
    adzed by a grubbing hoe for the stocks or the docks,
    more prized for all those gashes—
    that *right roughness* you admire,
    your soul's facture—
    I get it, but—really? A rather
    wooden translation of donning
    sackcloth and ashes?

    "Me? I'm aiming myself like an arrow smack
    at the black hole bull's-eye
    heart of the star shire, apple
    of God's eye, the O
    that first spike poked
    in Christ's palm, through which
    sinners who repent may enter Heaven."

'Mercy? *Johnny*. More like you to dance
Mad Maud barefoot across
the Brigg o' Dread—the Pont
Neuf in your head—to requite
the love she gave the Lord, and join
the left bank with the right
hemisphere of your brain,
hard-wire it in, then storm
Heaven in the rain.'

That phone call, you found
a new way to get
the last word: three days later,
you were dead.

Your war came up.
You said,

> "Commie, pinko, red!—
> Rice is their daily bread!
> —License to kill them dead?
> Fucking Marco Polo!
> Look. Paris is a mistress,
> Rome's the wife
> you love a lifetime.
> Whatever foxhole you fall into,
> kid, keep it civil.
> When in Rome—
> *cum Romano Romanus eris*—
> just the same as ferrous
> oxide, never sleep."

'Fer*ric*—'

"Never doubt—"

'Objection!'

> "Overruled!
> Two will get you twenty—
> step in Heaven, you'll have plenty
> Shantih Shantih Shantih
> to argue *Good v. Evil*.
> When in Hell, French kiss the devil.
> Plead *nolo*, at law
> and equity, but not
> to God. You never
> heard it from me.
> Over and out."

In the silence after
you clicked off, I thought:
Johnny, don't be caught
dead among souls stuck
on the bank of the Styx,
lacking Charon's tax,
toll for the crossing.
Trump Hades at the last,
redeem the obol tucked
upright atop your tongue
with unleavened
bread, the risen
Christ in the pyx,
viaticum, provision
for the road ahead.

*

Ten years ago, shooting
the shit in a duck blind
on a salt marsh at first light,
you said when you died
you wanted your casket to match
the gunmetal skies.

"Ah, Johnny. Noon or midnight?" I asked.
"Blue? Or Parkerize?"

*

Sunshine ignites your wife's
eyes, her cobalt
palmprint on the coffin.
Brass hinges glint,
squinting in a brief
and final brightness.

Corragio, brave heart!
The box is lowered on straps
into the hole.
The priest signs the air
above you with a cross.
Your widow leans to drop
a poppy after you.
Handfuls of clay and mud
spatter the casket lid, I read
signs of the Lord's dominion everywhere.
Give us some sign, Lord, of your covenant
with Noah after the flood
when your rainbow
flamed the air.
                      Do you still
promise what you promised? Or will
all those seas and rivers Noah crossed
whelm us again?

The year I made my first
communion, Easter lilies blew
resurrexit through
white trumpets, tungsten stamens blazed
fifty days and nights through Pentecost.

They did. I know they did—I saw—
I swear! I saw—I heard—
my own ears and eyes.

Churches closed for Covid,
this past Easter, I missed—
look! That hawk's

locking on a pigeon! O, my poor
cousin to the dove that brought
God's olive branch to man—

mid-air strike, Johnny! Feathers
iridesce, drift down to gloss
Isaiah and the waters where they drown.

Talons grip the trefoil
knob that crowns the cross
atop St. Aidan's steeple.

Lamb of God,
a redtail's roosting on your crucifix.

Whose sunlight sizzles down that lightning rod?

Notes

THE TWENTY-TWENTIETH YEAR OF OUR LORD

Hart Island, in the west end of Long Island Sound, has served as New York City's potter's field since 1869. With morgues filled and refrigerator trucks overflowing, in the rush to inter victims and limit the spread of Covid-19, many of the city's dead, including those with family—some temporarily, some erroneously—were buried here in mass graves. The island has also served as the site of a Civil War POW camp, a yellow fever quarantine hospital, tuberculosis sanatorium, women's psychiatric asylum, male reformatory, workhouse, prison, homeless shelter, and a battery of underground missile silos during the Cold War.

BOCA NEGRA

Boca Negra (Black Mouth) is the name of a canyon in Petroglyph National Monument on the mesa west of Albuquerque, New Mexico. The West Mesa was formed quite recently in geologic time from roughly 220,000–150,000 years ago, culminating in the eruption of six main lava flows from five volcanic cones formed atop the material produced by earlier volcanic activity. Those spatter and cinder cones are visible from the mesa above Boca Negra. Subsequent erosion of the softer substrate beneath the lava has left a seventeen-mile-long escarpment strewn with black basalt boulders broken away from the flows. The National Parks Service estimates that twenty-five thousand petroglyphs have been scratched into the basalt, mostly by Native Americans, but later by Hispanic and Anglo settlers. Archaeologists say the earliest images date back perhaps four thousand years; the Native tradition holds they are older still.

Black Ops: readers are familiar with this abbreviated name for covert operations, legal or otherwise, by military, paramilitary, private, or governmental groups where deniability is key: if you're captured, no one knows you; if you die, you have no homeland but the shadow of the body between your body and the earth on which it lies. Worth noting, in the landscape of this poem, *Boca Negra*, where Vulcan, Roman god of fire, is everywhere present but nowhere invoked: the epithet Black Ops calls up the Sabine goddess Ops (promoted to a Roman deity): earth goddess, goddess of fertility and plenty. As with other chthonic gods—Pluto included, god of the dead and the underworld, whose darkness brings forth riches and whose name betokens wealth—Ops's wealth and abundance are manifest in modern English words: copious, cornucopia, opus. Sister and wife to Saturn, she is known as Rhea in Greece, where she is married to $Κρονος$, the Titan who is Zeus's father, and who, since time immemorial, has been conflated with $Χρονος$, Time, the father who devours his children. Ops/Rhea saved Jupiter/Zeus from the fate of his siblings, and is honored as the mother of the gods. The phrase "black ops" emphasizes her dark, chthonic nature and makes of—better, discovers her opulence as—a darkness shining in brightness. Under this aspect, the greatest of the riches that this goddess offers is self-knowledge, though that advancement of learning may come at considerable personal cost.

Anno Domini 1999
delenda est Carthago: Carthage must be destroyed.

Lupus est homo homini: man is a wolf to man.

Omertà: code of silence, especially as required (and enforced) by the Mafia.

Petra
Petra is the ancient Nabataean city in Jordan.

Can't Anyone Untie Us?
The title is taken from *Capricho* № 75 of Goya's *Los Caprichos*: ¿No hay quien nos desate?

Morpho
hic jacet: here lies

Winterreise
Winter Journey: Franz Schubert's song cycle for voice and piano, setting poems by Wilhelm Müller; four years earlier, he had composed a song cycle for Müller's group of poems titled *Die Schöne Müllerin* (The Miller's Beautiful Daughter or The Maid of the Mill). Schubert completed *Winterreise* in 1827, the year before he died at thirty-one.

Tetragrammaton
The title refers to the four Hebrew letters of God's name, which we pronounce as Yahweh or Jehovah, in violation of the Biblical prohibition against speaking or writing the full name of God. On God's distance and silence, Simone Weil is eloquent:

> *It is God who in love withdraws from us so that we can love him. For if we were exposed to the direct radiance of his love, without the protection of space, of time and of matter, we should be evaporated like water in the sun; there would not be enough 'I' in us to make it possible to surrender the 'I' for love's sake.*
>
> *The speech of created beings is with sounds. The word of God is silence. . . . The whole of creation is nothing but its vibration.*

Metamorphosis
Bombyx mori: domesticated silk moth whose larval (silkworm) stages feed on the leaves of the mulberry (L. *morus, mori*). The female lays eggs which hatch into larvae that undergo four molts and five *instars* (stages of development), finally wrapping themselves in cocoons of raw silk which protect them during their transformation into pupae and through the completion of their metamorphosis from which they emerge as adults or imagoes—silk moths. Unlike their wild relatives,

domesticated silk moths can neither feed nor fly; they mate, females lay eggs, then females and males die, three to six days after having emerged from the cocoon.

morituri te salutamus: We who are about to die salute you. Suetonius wrote that gladiators at the Fucine Lake addressed Emperor Claudius with these words before the start of the show—a mock naval battle featuring combat to the death (real)—they were presenting for his vivid entertainment.

Acknowledgments

Grateful acknowledgment is given to Arrowsmith Press, publisher of the chapbook *Black Ops* (2018), and to the following print and online journals and magazines where many of these poems first appeared, some in different form or under a different title: *The New Yorker, A Public Space, Little Star, Agni, Consequence, Ep;phany,* as well as to the W. B. Yeats Society of New York website for featuring work from this book. Thanks also to Poetry Daily for showcasing "Perfect Match."

Acknowledgment is made with gratitude to the Massachusetts Cultural Council for the support of an Artist Fellowship while some of these poems were being written.

Thanks to Askold Melnyczuk, and to Ezra Fox, who designed and typeset the book, for making a pleasure of preparing this collection for print.

I thank Kai Maristed and Jeffrey Gustavson for their generous, gloves-off readings of these poems in manuscript. And thank you, Gus, for our decades-long, ongoing conversation in—and out of—poems.

Photo by Kai Maristed

Martin Edmunds' poems have appeared in *Agni, The New Yorker, A Public Space, The Paris Review, Little Star, The Nation, The Partisan Review, Southwest Review,* Berfrois, and *Consequence* among other journals, and are featured on Poetry Daily and the Yeats Society of NY website. His chapbook *Black Ops* was published by Arrowsmith Press; his book *The High Road to Taos* won the National Poetry Series competition. His work appears in *The Arvon Anthology* (Ted Hughes and Seamus Heaney (Eds.), *Under 35: The New Generation of American Poets,* and *New Mexico Poetry Renaissance: A Community on Paper*. Edmunds was for several years an Artist-in-Residence at the Cathedral of Saint John the Divine; other honors include an Artist Fellowship from the Massachusetts Cultural Council, the "Discovery"/The Nation Prize, and the Lloyd McKim Garrison Medal for Poetry. He co-wrote the screenplay for the feature *Passion in the Desert* (Roland Films/Fine Line), an adaptation of the Balzac story. Edmunds freelances as a writer and editor, teaches privately, and vies publicly with moon snails, sea stars, and gulls for clams and oysters.

ARROWSMITH is named after the late William Arrowsmith, a renowned classics scholar, literary and film critic. General editor of thirty-three volumes of *The Greek Tragedy in New Translations*, he was also a brilliant translator of Eugenio Montale, Cesare Pavese, and others. Arrowsmith, who taught for years in Boston University's University Professors Program, championed not only the classics and the finest in contemporary literature, he was also passionate about the importance of recognizing the translator's role in bringing the original work to life in a new language.

Like the arrowsmith who turns his arrows straight and true,
a wise person makes his character straight and true.

— Buddha

Books by
ARROWSMITH PRESS

Girls by Oksana Zabuzhko
Bula Matari/Smasher of Rocks by Tom Sleigh
This Carrying Life by Maureen McLane
Cries of Animal Dying by Lawrence Ferlinghetti
Animals in Wartime by Matiop Wal
Divided Mind by George Scialabba
The Jinn by Amira El-Zein
Bergstein edited by Askold Melnyczuk
Arrow Breaking Apart by Jason Shinder
Beyond Alchemy by Daniel Berrigan
*Conscience, Consequence: Reflections on
Father Daniel Berrigan* edited by Askold Melnyczuk
Ric's Progress by Donald Hall
Return To The Sea by Etnairis Rivera
The Kingdom of His Will by Catherine Parnell
Eight Notes from the Blue Angel by Marjana Savka
Fifty-Two by Melissa Green
Music In—And On—The Air by Lloyd Schwartz
Magpiety by Melissa Green
Reality Hunger by William Pierce
Soundings: On The Poetry of Melissa Green edited by Sumita Chakraborty
The Corny Toys by Thomas Sayers Ellis
Black Ops by Martin Edmunds
Museum of Silence by Romeo Oriogun
City of Water by Mitch Manning
Passeggiate by Judith Baumel
Persephone Blues by Oksana Lutsyshyna
The Uncollected Delmore Schwartz edited by Ben Mazer
The Light Outside by George Kovach
The Blood of San Gennaro by Scott Harney edited by Megan Marshall
No Sign by Peter Balakian
Firebird by Kythe Heller
The Selected Poems of Oksana Zabuzhko edited by Askold Melnyczuk
The Age of Waiting by Douglas J. Penick
Manimal Woe by Fanny Howe
Crank Shaped Notes by Thomas Sayers Ellis
The Land of Mild Light by Rafael Cadenas edited by Nidia Hernández
The Silence of Your Name by Alexandra Marshall